Where Would We Be Without Our HONEY BEES?

Author: Elle Ryan
Illustrator: Famsu Illustration

Look! There are some honey bees!
They love to fly through the trees.
Buzz, buzz, buzz.

Let's follow them!

They're headed toward those flowers!
Can you see what they are doing?
Yes, they are collecting nectar and pollen.

Look at those little pollen
baskets on their legs.
Too cute!

Let's follow them again...

They are flying back to their hive.
To their mum.

She's called the 'queen bee', and she loves to be in charge. She sits on her throne and demands what work has to be done.
The worker bees busily fill the hive with the nectar and pollen they have collected from the flowers.

But what for?

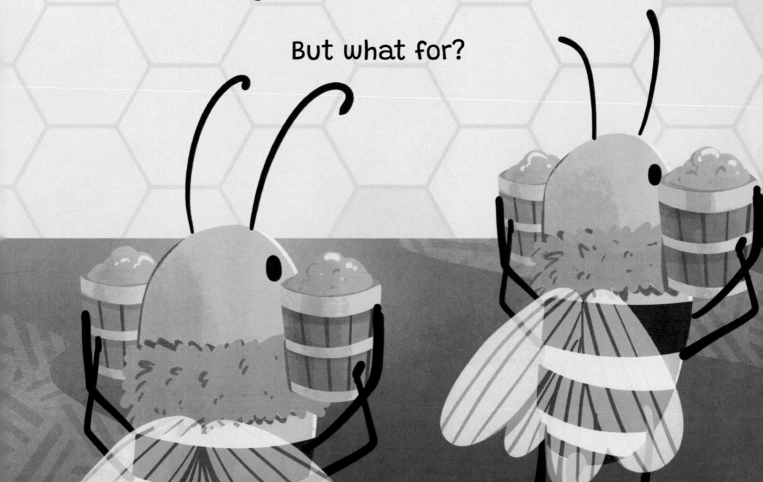

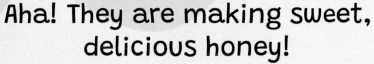

Aha! They are making sweet, delicious honey!

They are very clever. The nectar and pollen are transformed with the help of an enzyme in the bee's tummy.

Not long after, the honeycomb hive turns it into honey.

The queen does other important things — like starting the whole colony by laying her eggs and carefully placing them in the honeycomb hive!

After three days, the eggs change into larvae that wiggle and wriggle about inside their hexagon-shaped house.

The worker bees continue to feed the larvae with pollen and nectar they have collected.

After six days, they cover the honeycomb in a cocoon, and the wiggly larvae turn into pupas — that's how they prepare their bodies for flight.

Wow! It's been twelve days, and something is happening!

Something is coming out!

Yes, brand new bees!

The antennae have grown, and the body
has changed colour; it's now yellow and
black.

The pupa's wings are newly formed and almost ready for their first flight.

Oh, look! They are standing in line while the queen bee points her staff. She's handing out jobs for her children.

"Come here, my magnificent baby bee," she says to one particular bee.

"You will go back to the nursery and live with the nurse bees, for you will be the one to become the future queen!"

Wow, that bee is lucky!

The queen bee is now pointing her staff
to the group on the left and says,

"A worker bee you shall be.
So, prepare your sting and grab your pollen baskets
to gather nectar and pollen.

The rest of you are strong but have no sting.
You will stay close to the hive and look after me;
therefore, you shall be drone bees."

And now that spring has sprung,
the bees are extra busy.
Let's watch them again!

The honey bees seem to love the bright
sunny days and fresh flowered blooms,
don't they?

They fly from plant to plant gathering nectar and pollen.
They have a big job: filling their pollen baskets.

Their queen will be very happy.

While the bees land on each flower, they are pollinating the flower too, and that means the fruit can grow.

That apple tree over there needs five bees to pollinate it, and the growing apple needs bee pollination for each seed.

If the bees miss or simply forget, the apple grows a little wonky.

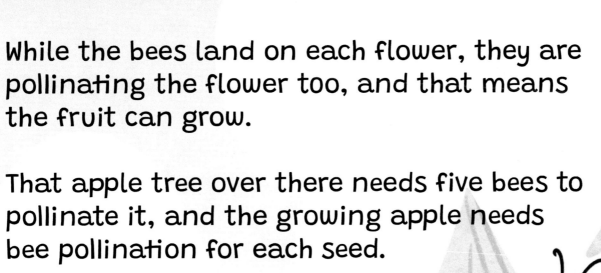

That bee was close! But don't worry, bees don't go out of their way to sting you.

They only sting if they are scared, like if you step on them. You would be scared too if someone stepped on you!

So, always watch where you are walking when there are bees around.
And if one is too close, stay calm. If you get scared and scream, they might get frightened and be more likely to sting.
We know the sting hurts and contains bee venom, but the bees only sting if they really have to, because they do not survive after using their sting.

So, it's a good idea to avoid bees, isn't it?
Because we also need our bees!

Did you know that bees are not just interesting,
cute, buzzing insects, but they are essential
for our ecosystem? Without bees,
we wouldn't have the food we love to eat!

If you see bees nearby, watch them from a distance, they have a big, important job to do.

Next time you pour that golden honey onto your pancakes or bite into a juicy apple, take a moment to think about how wonderful it is, and remember it took the hard work of many bees to make it so.

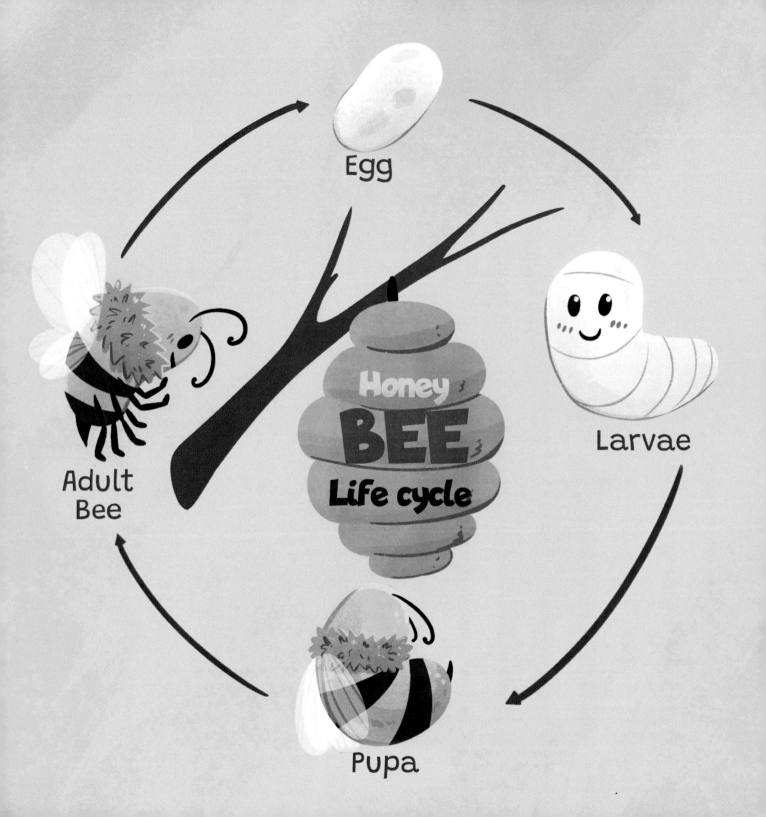

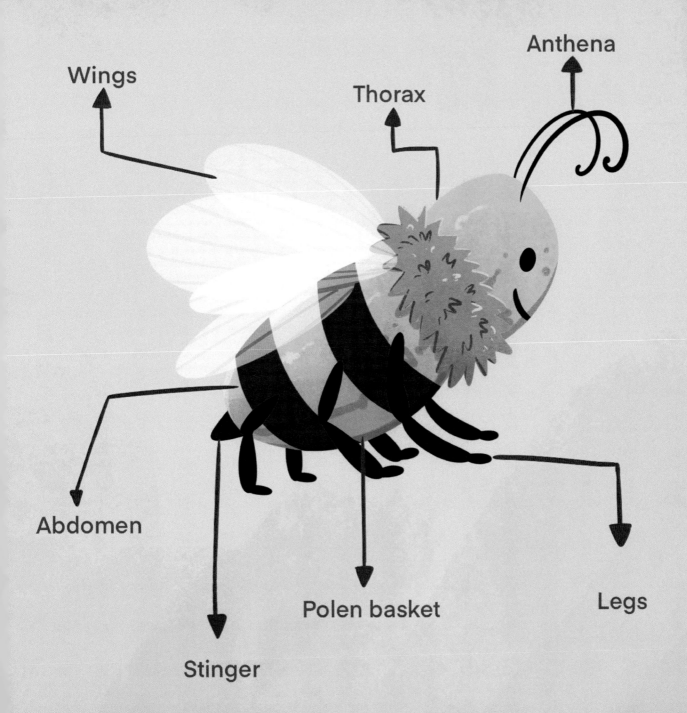

Wings

Thorax

Anthena

Abdomen

Stinger

Polen basket

Legs

Made in the USA
Las Vegas, NV
17 December 2024